Terrific
TRAINS

For Mandy, John, Chloe and Charlie – T.M.
For Gorran – A.P.

First published 1998 by Kingfisher
First published in paperback 2000 by Kingfisher
This edition published 2013 by Macmillan Children's Books
a division of Macmillan Publishers Limited
20 New Wharf Road, London N1 9RR
Basingstoke and Oxford
Associated companies throughout the world

www.panmacmillan.com

ISBN: 978-1-4472-1269-0

Text copyright © Tony Mitton 1998
Illustrations copyright © Ant Parker 1998

Moral rights asserted.

3 5 7 9 8 6 4 2

A CIP catalogue record for this book is available from the British Library.

Printed in China

Terrific
TRAINS

Tony Mitton
and
Ant Parker

MACMILLAN CHILDREN'S BOOKS

Big trains, small trains, old trains and new,

rattling and whistling – choo, choo, choo!

Starting from the station with a whistle and a hiss

steam trains puffing and chuffing like this.

Diesel trains rushing as they rattle down the line,

warning us they're coming with a long, low whine.

Metal wheels whirl as they whizz along the track.
They shimmer and they swish
with a slick click-clack.

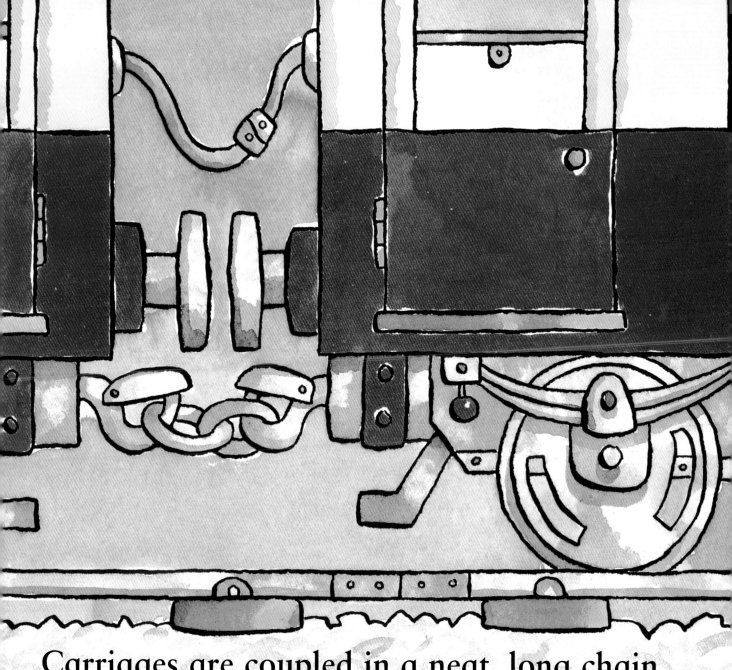

Carriages are coupled in a neat, long chain.
An engine pulls the carriages,
and that makes a train.

If a train meets a river or a valley or a ridge,

the train goes over on a big, strong bridge.

If a train meets a mountain it doesn't have to stop

It travels through a tunnel and your ears go pop!

When too many trains try to share the same track,

the signals and the points have to hold some back.

When the rail meets a road,
there's a crossing with a gate.

The train rushes through
while the traffic has to wait.

Trains travel anytime, even very late.

This train's delivering a big load of freight.

This train's for passengers.
We'll soon be on our way.

All aboard and wave goodbye –
we're off on holiday!

Train bits

rails

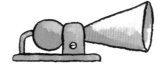

electric rail

these are metal strips that form a pathway called a **track** or **railway line** – some trains get their power from an electric rail

whistle

this makes a noise to warn everyone that the train is coming

wagon

this is for carrying goods, called **freight**

signal

this tells train drivers when to stop and go

carriage

this is for carrying people, called **passengers**

points

these are rails that move to let the railway line divide so the train changes direction